EXPANDING AMERICA

The California Gold Rush

Kate Shoup

Cavendish Square
New York

Published in 2016 by Cavendish Square Publishing, LLC
243 5th Avenue, Suite 136, New York, NY 10016

First Edition

Website: cavendishsq.com

CPSIA Compliance Information: Batch #CW16CSQ

Library of Congress Cataloging-in-Publication Data

Shoup, Kate, 1972- author.
The California gold rush / Kate Shoup.
pages cm. — (Expanding America)
Includes bibliographical references and index.
ISBN 978-1-5026-0968-7 (hardcover) ISBN 978-1-5026-0969-4 (ebook)
1. California—Gold discoveries—Juvenile literature. 2. California—History—1846-1850—Juvenile literature. 3. Gold miners—California—History—19th century—Juvenile literature. 4. Frontier and pioneer life—California—Juvenile literature. I. Title.

F865.S5515 2016
979.4'04—dc23

2015034508

Editorial Director: David McNamara
Editors: Andrew Coddington and Kelly Spence
Copy Editor: Rebecca Rohan
Art Director: Jeffrey Talbot
Designers: Amy Greenan and Stephanie Flecha
Senior Production Manager: Jennifer Ryder-Talbot
Production Editor: Renni Johnson
Photo Research: J8 Media

The photographs in this book are used by permission and through the courtesy of: Library of Congress Prints and Photographs Division, Washington, D.C., cover; map, front, back covers and throughout the book; SSPL/Getty Images, 5; Ritu Manoj Jethani/Shutterstock.com, 6; MPI/Getty Images, 11; William Toti (http://www.flickr.com/people/24039321@N07) File: Mission San Diego de Alcala.jpg - Wikimedia Commons, 13; Universal Images Group/Getty Images, 15; Devin Cook/File: Flag of California.svg - Wikimedia Commons, 19; © Giggette/File: Alta California (location map scheme). svg Wikimedia Commons, 22; Heritage/Superstock, 24; Collection of the New-York Historical Society, USA/Bridgeman Images, 27; Underwood Archives/Getty Images, 28; Brickey/File: Prospector in the desert with horse and two burros, 1880-1910 (CHS-1410).jpg - Wikimedia Commons, 35; North Wind Picture Archives, 38; Universal History Archive/UIG via Getty Images, 45; Library of Congress Prints and Photographs Division, Washington, D.C./File: San Francisco harbor 1851 c sharp.jpg - Wikimedia Commons, 47; Visions of America/UIG via Getty Images, 54; Huntington Library/Superstock, 56; Hulton Archive/Getty Images, 59; By California Constitutional Convention of 1849 [Public domain or Public domain], File: California Constitution 1849 title page.jpg via Wikimedia Commons, 65; Hulton Archive/Getty Images, 69; Everett Historical/Shutterstock, 72; Mary Park Seavy Benton (1815-1910)/California Historical Society/Gift of Clara L. Watson/Bridgeman Images, 76; Library of Congress Prints and Photographs Division Washington, D.C., File: Historic American Buildings Survey Roger Sturtevant, Photo. Sierra County, CA HABS CAL,46-DOWNV.V,1-1.tif - Wikimedia Commons, 78; Andrew J. Russell [Public domain], Yale University Libraries via Wikimedia Commons, 80.

Printed in the United States of America

CONTENTS

INTRODUCTION

All That Glitters

The California Gold Rush marked a turning point in American history. In the words of historian H. W. Brands, the discovery of gold in California was, "a seminal event in history, one of those rare moments that divide human existence into before and after." It would have an enormous effect on the **prospectors** who searched for gold, the region of California, the United States as a whole, and the entire world.

In 2014, California boasted a population of over 38 million—more than any other state in the Union. But this was not always the case. When California became **annexed** by the United States in 1848, fewer than 12,000 settlers of white or Mexican descent lived in the area. The Native American population is unknown, but is estimated to have been about 150,000.

What caused this population explosion? No doubt there were many factors. But clearly the California Gold Rush, which lasted from 1848 until 1855, played a significant role. All told, some three hundred thousand people migrated to California during this period, laying the foundation for further growth in the years to come.

Before the annexation of California in 1848, the Native American population in the area was much higher.

The California Gold Rush did more than launch, in Brands's words, "the most astonishing mass movement of people since the Crusades." The discovery of gold in the Sierra Nevada mountain range helped to "initiate the modern era of American economic development." Thanks to the Gold Rush, and the ensuing shift in population, new markets opened up in the United States and abroad. And of course, more gold meant more wealth, which in turn spurred trade and investments.

There was a less-tangible effect, too. Before, as noted by Brand, the American dream was "the dream of the Puritans … of men and women content to accumulate their modest fortunes a little at a time, year by year by year." But the California Gold Rush changed all that. As a result of discovering gold, "The new dream was the dream of instant wealth, won in a twinkling by audacity and good luck." In this way, the Gold Rush was a great equalizer. Especially in the early years of the California Gold Rush, any person with a pan and a pick could dig for gold. Anyone could strike it rich! This new sense of economic mobility would soon permeate American culture.

Juan Rodriguez Cabrillo, the first European explorer to land in modern-day California

CHAPTER ONE

A Brief History of California

Although the California Gold Rush did not begin until 1848, the hunt for gold had long been a part of the region's history. Indeed, it was the search for gold that led the first European explorers to the area. These men were following stories of a province called Cibola. Rumored to exist far to the northwest, Cibola was believed to abound with gold and other valuable minerals.

The first of these European explorers was Juan Rodriguez Cabrillo, a Portuguese **conquistador** who had settled in New Spain. In 1542, the Spanish crown commissioned Cabrillo to sail north from his home in what is now Guatemala to search for Cibola, as well as for a northern passage from the Pacific to the Atlantic. On September 28, 1542, Cabrillo "discovered" present-day California—although, to be fair, indigenous people had lived there for thousands of years—

landing in what is now San Diego. From there, Cabrillo sailed northward, turning back at Port Reyes, roughly 30 miles (48 kilometers) north of present-day San Francisco.

During the voyage, Cabrillo claimed territory along the California coast for Spain. However, his search for Cibola and for a northern passage proved fruitless. Nor did Cabrillo, who died on the expedition after a broken leg turned gangrenous, find much in the way of what the Spaniards considered advanced Native civilizations or significant agriculture. In other words, there was nothing in California for Spain to exploit. Therefore, California was of little use to the Spanish crown. For the time being, the area was ignored.

Sir Francis Drake Establishes Nova Albion

It would be more than thirty years before another European set eyes on California. This time, it was an Englishman—Sir Francis Drake. On November 15, 1577, Drake, leading a fleet of five ships with some 164 men, departed by sea from Plymouth, England, on a voyage to **circumnavigate** the globe.

En route, Drake sailed the California coast. In June of 1579, his party came ashore near Port Reyes. Although the territory had been claimed for Spain by Cabrillo some thirty years earlier, Drake appropriated it for England. Perhaps Drake was unaware of Cabrillo's claim. According to Francis Pretty, a member of Drake's party, "It seemeth that the Spaniards hitherto had never been in this part of the country, neither did ever discover the land by many degrees to the southwards of this place." In any case, Drake named the region Nova Albion—*Nova* meaning "new" and *Albion* being a poetic term for England.

What's In a Name?

Even before Cabrillo explored the area, Spaniards referred to the region as California. The origin of this name is unclear. Some believe it comes from the Latin *calida fornax*, meaning "hot oven." Others say it stems from a Native word meaning "high hill." A more likely explanation, however, is that the name California comes from a novel by Spanish writer Garcí Ordónez de Montalvo. First published in 1510, the fanciful tale, called *Las Sergas de Esplandian* (*The Adventures of Esplandian*), described an island called California, located "on the right hand of the Indies, very near to the Terrestrial Paradise." The island was "peopled with black women, without any men among them." According to the story, California was ruled by "a Queen, large of body, very beautiful, in the prime of her years." (Incidentally, the story also noted that the island was populated by griffins—mythical creatures with the head and wings of an eagle and the body of a lion.)

Like Cabrillo before him, Drake believed there was gold in the area. As noted by Pretty, "There is no part of earth here to be taken up, wherein there is not some probable show of gold or silver." Drake, however, did not seek it out. Instead, he and his party left the area shortly after arriving

The Native People of California

The Europeans were hardly the first people to arrive in California. The land had long been settled by Native American tribes. Members of these tribes were in turn descendants of earlier civilizations dating back more than twelve thousand years. These early inhabitants likely reached the area by crossing a land bridge that once connected what is now the Bering Strait between Asia and North America.

When the Europeans first arrived in California, its inhabitants—total population estimates range between three hundred thousand and seven hundred thousand people—were members of more than one hundred Native American tribes. These included the Cahuilleno, Chumash, Karok, Maidu, Miwok, Modoc, Mojave, Ohlone, Pomo, Paiute, Serrano, Shasta, Tataviam, Tongya, Wintu, and Yokuts tribes.

Some of these tribes resisted the arrival of the Europeans. Others were friendly. These included the indigenous people who greeted Sir Francis Drake near modern-day Port Reyes, likely members of the Miwok tribe. According to Francis Pretty, "The people of the country… shewed themselves unto us, and sent a present to our General." He continued, "The presents which they sent to

Native Americans in traditional costume

our General, were feathers, and cauls of network." Pretty went on to describe these Native people, noting that "The men go naked; the women take bulrushes, and kemb them after the manner of hemp, and thereof make their loose garments, which being knit about their middles, hang down about their hips, having also about their shoulders a skin of deer, with the hair upon it."

Ancestors of these Native peoples still live in California today, although their numbers are greatly diminished. Many Native Americans perished from new diseases introduced by the Europeans after first contact. Others starved as they were driven off their traditional hunting, fishing, and food-gathering grounds. Still more were slain by Europeans and, later, Americans, who sought to claim their lands.

and continued on their route around the globe—a journey they would complete in 1580.

The Spanish Return

In 1602, another Spanish explorer sailed the coast of present-day California: Sebastián Vizcaíno. He made it as far as Monterey Bay before turning back. Still, Spain chose not to colonize the area, which it called Alta California. (This is in contrast to the Mexican state of Baja California, which is part of present-day Mexico.) That changed in 1769.

Why the change? There were a number of reasons. First was the growing influence of Great Britain over North America. Although England had never settled Nova Albion, it had colonized the eastern portion of North America. It had also claimed present-day Canada after its victory over the French in the Seven Years' War. Second was the threat of Russia, which had established a presence in Alaska—and with it, a lucrative fur trade.

To prevent territory in Alta California from falling into British or Russian hands, Spain sought to establish **missions** in the region. These missions were settlements built to gain a foothold in the area as well as to convert the Native people to Christianity. The first of these was the Mission San Diego de Alcala, completed in July of 1769. Eventually, Spain built twenty-one missions. These settlements were usually populated by a handful of priests and soldiers and maintained by local Natives (who, for all practical purposes, were treated as slaves). They dotted the coast from San Diego to San Francisco, which was then called Yerba Buena. Each mission was roughly 30 miles (48 km) from the next, or one day's ride on horseback. They were linked by a trail called the El Camino Real.

In addition to these missions, Spain constructed **presidios**, or forts, in Alta California. The first of these

The Mission San Diego de Alcala in San Diego

was the Presidio of San Diego, established in May 1769. Three more soon followed, strategically placed along the California coast in Yerba Buena, Santa Barbara, and Sonoma. Each of these was manned by between ten and one hundred men.

To support these missions and presidios, Spanish settlers established six towns called **pueblos**: Los Angeles, San Diego, Yerba Buena, Santa Barbara, Villa de Branciforte (which later became Santa Cruz), and San Jose. Spain also issued large land grants, called **ranchos**, to prospective settlers. Each rancho covered 35,000 acres (14,164 hectares), and most who settled on these lands devoted themselves to raising cattle, horses, and sheep.

California Under Mexican Rule

In May 1808, French leader Napoleon Bonaparte forced King Carlos IV of Spain to abdicate the Spanish throne.

Junípero Serra

Leading the charge to establish the mission system in Alta California was Catholic priest Junípero Serra. He was born to a humble family on the island of Mallorca off the coast of Spain. As a teenager, Serra was ordained as a priest, and at twenty-four, he became a professor of theology, later accepting a post at the prestigious Lullian University. Despite his success, however, Serra longed for something more.

In 1749, Serra traveled to Mexico City, the capital of New Spain. There, he spent the next several years working as a professor at the College of San Fernando. In addition, he took on work as a **missionary**.

Serra found his true calling in 1767. That year, Emperor Carlos III of Spain exiled the **Jesuits** from New Spain. The Jesuits were a group of Catholic priests who traveled the world to perform missionary work—that is, to spread Christianity to Native people. In doing so, this group had also accrued substantial assets and power, making them a clear threat to the emperor.

As a result of the Jesuits' expulsion, the missions they had established sat neglected. Who would take their place? Enter the order of **Franciscans**, of which Serra was a member. Like the Jesuits, the Franciscans were known for their missionary work. When asked by the Spanish government to take over the Jesuit missions, these priests,

Father Junípero Serra, who founded the mission chain in Alta California

including Serra, readily agreed. Serra was named the head of a series of missions that had been built by the Jesuit order in the Mexican state of Baja California.

The next year, he was asked to build the mission system in Alta California. By then, Serra was fifty years old, very thin and asthmatic, and had a severely injured leg. Nevertheless, he agreed. Serra led the foundation of the mission in San Diego and went on to personally establish eight others.

Serra died in 1784 at the age of seventy. He was beatified, meaning the Catholic Church confirmed his ascension into heaven, by Pope John Paul II in 1988. In September 2015, Pope Francis officially canonized Serra during his visit to Washington, DC, making him a saint.

Naturally, chaos in Spain meant there was little oversight of its colonies in the New World.

In 1810, in the face of this chaos, revolutionaries in Mexico—which was part of New Spain—saw their chance to rise up. Led by a Catholic priest named Miguel Hidalgo, Mexican rebels sought independence from Spain. Although Hidalgo, who would later be known as the Father of Mexico, was executed by Spanish forces in 1811, his efforts successfully launched the Mexican War for Independence.

The Mexican War for Independence lasted a decade. In 1821, Mexico defeated Spain and gained its independence. It also gained Spain's territory in North America, including Alta California. At that time, the territory consisted of all of present-day California and Arizona, as well as parts of Nevada and Utah.

Although Spain had made a substantial effort to settle Alta California, its population remained relatively small, so when it came under Mexican rule, the government simply called it a territory rather than naming it a state. Given its small population and, therefore, its low tax revenues—not to mention its distance from the new nation's capital, Mexico City—Alta Vista was a mere blip on the radar of the Mexican government. That's not to say the territory lacked supervision, however. A series of governors oversaw the area. Typically, these men came from Mexico City rather than Alta California.

The mission system in California decayed under Mexican rule. This was in part due to the General Law of Expulsion, passed by the Mexican Congress in 1827, which deemed all residents of Mexico born in Spain to be illegal immigrants. Under that law, they were ordered to leave, including many of the clergy who served the missions in Alta California. The missions were further undermined by a second law, called

"An Act for the Secularization of the Missions of California," passed in 1833. Lawmakers passed this law to appease the soldiers, ranchers, and farmers in Alta California who coveted the rich coastal lands controlled by the missions. By 1846, the law had done its work, with all mission lands—some 8,600,000 acres (3,480,296 ha) in all—having been placed in private hands.

In 1836, Alta California became a Mexican state—or, actually, half of one. Mexican officials merged Alta California with Baja California to form a single department, which it called California. This change had little effect on Alta California, however. It remained the distant outpost it had always been.

That changed in 1841. That year, the Mexican government became aware of a growing threat from the United States, which had come to believe it was entitled to the lands located to its west. In response, the president of Mexico, Antonio López de Santa Anna, deployed three hundred troops to Alta California in 1842. These were led by Brigadier General Manuel Micheltorena, who was to assume the governorship upon arrival in the region.

The **Californios**—the name given to the Spanish-speaking people of Alta California—were unhappy with this choice. Micheltorena, like so many governors before him, was an outsider. The Californios wanted to install one of their own people as governor. In November 1844, the Californios, backed by wealthy landowners, rebelled. Micheltorena quickly negotiated a truce with the rebels, promising to dismiss his troops. He then backed out of the deal. This proved unwise. Micheltorena and his troops were defeated by the Californios in February 1845 at the Battle of Providencia, north of Los Angeles. Micheltorena had no choice but to surrender his governorship and leave Alta California with his troops.

The Mexican-American War and the Annexation of California

Alta California would soon become involved in a new conflict: the Mexican-American War, which began on May 13, 1846. At the root of the conflict was a dispute between Mexico and the United States over the state of Texas. Texas had seceded from Mexico in 1836 and declared its independence during the Texas Revolution. Mexico, however, refused to acknowledge the new republic's sovereignty. Tensions rose nine years later, after the annexation of Texas by the United States, at which time Texas became the twenty-eighth state in the Union. From Mexico's point of view, Texas was still its property—and it was property worth fighting for. After multiple attacks by Mexican troops on American soldiers along the Texas–Mexico border, the United States declared war.

The war was not merely about the defense of Texas, however. For the United States, there were other motives. One was its belief in **manifest destiny**, or the philosophy that it was America's right—indeed, its duty—to expand its territory and its way of life to the Pacific Ocean, and beyond. This view quickly became evident during the course of the Mexican-American War when the fighting expanded beyond the Texas-Mexico border. In fact, American settlers in Alta California took action against Mexico even before they learned that war had been declared.

On June 14, one month after Congress's declaration of war, but several weeks before official word arrived in the region (there were no railways, steamships, or telegraph wires in the area yet), thirty-four American settlers in the Sacramento Valley seized control of Sonoma, an undefended Mexican outpost. This was in response to a rumor that General José Castro, the senior Mexican military

The flag for the California Republic. This flag remains in use today, as the state flag.

officer in Alta California, was gathering an army to expel them from the area. One rebel, William Todd, designed a flag featuring the words "California Republic" beneath a star and a grizzly bear, which was hoisted over Sonoma. Thereafter, the rebels were called Bear Flaggers, and the land they occupied became known as Bear Flag Republic.

On July 2, the Bear Flaggers took over Yerba Buena. There, they joined forces with a group led by John C. Frémont. Frémont had been surveying the Oregon Territory. When he learned war between the United States and Mexico was imminent, he and his party headed for Alta California. Frémont's men, along with the Bear Flaggers, united to form the California Battalion, to be led by Frémont. Still, official word about the declaration of war had not yet arrived. Frémont was not acting under military orders, but operating under his own authority.

Around the same time, Commodore John D. Sloat, commander of the US Navy's Pacific Squadron, reached nearby Monterey by sea. He had been instructed to take the San Francisco Bay and to cordon off various Alta California ports when he was certain the war had begun. Sloat, assuming that Frémont was acting on orders from Washington, took Monterey on July 7. "Henceforth

Manifest Destiny

In 1811, John Quincy Adams, who would later become president of the United States, wrote, "The whole continent of North America appears to be destined by Divine Providence to be peopled by one nation, speaking one language, professing one general system of religious and political principles, and accustomed to one general tenor of social usages and customs." This view, referred to as continentalism, was quickly gaining traction among Americans.

In 1845, John L. O'Sullivan, the editor of an influential magazine called the *Democratic Review*, coined a new term to describe this ideology: manifest destiny. He wrote that it was "the fulfillment of our manifest destiny to overspread the continent allotted by Providence for the free development of our yearly multiplying millions."

Inherent in this view were two key points. First, the American people and their institutions held special virtues. (This is often referred to—even today—as American exceptionalism.) Second, it was both the destiny and the duty of the United States to remake the American West in its own image. Simply put, according to author Reginald Horsman, Americans believed themselves to be "innately superior" and "destined to bring good government, commercial prosperity, and Christianity to the American continents and the world."

Of course, spreading west often meant encroaching on lands that were already held by Native people. This did not give the Americans pause. As noted by Horsman, manifest destiny held that so-called inferior races "were doomed to subordinate status or extinction." Indeed, due to manifest destiny, several groups of Native peoples were simply killed. Others were force to settle in Indian Territory, in what is now Oklahoma.

Eventually, the notion of manifest destiny would evolve to include overseas expansion, as evidenced by the annexation of the Republic of Hawaii in 1898. "It is manifest destiny," President William McKinley said of the move. Later, the phrase "manifest destiny" would be used to describe America's belief that it is obligated to promote and preserve democracy abroad, a belief many Americans still hold today.

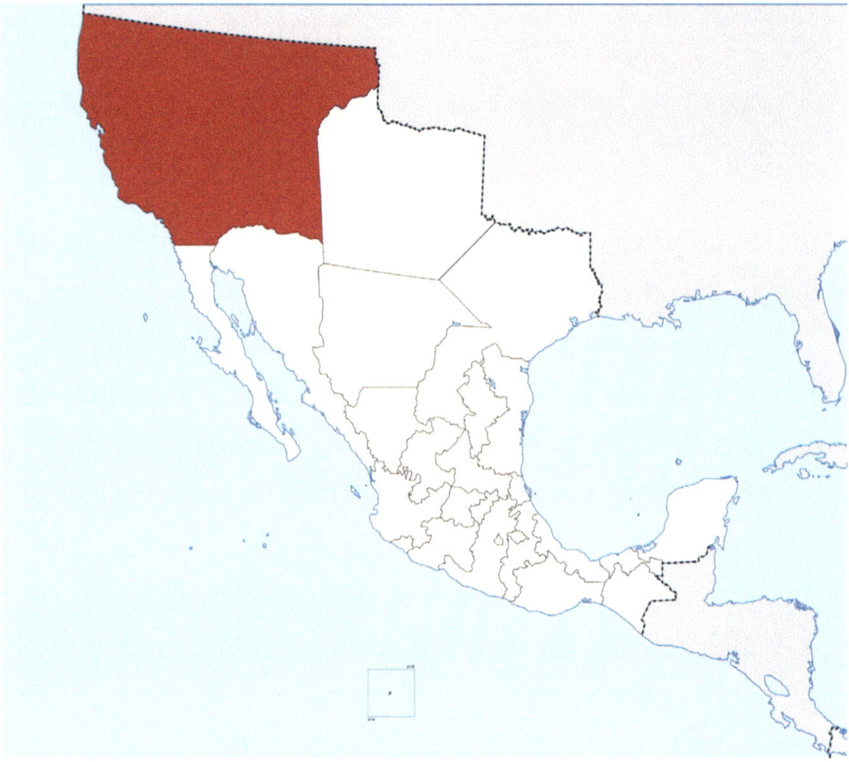

Alta California is the area in red. The region encompassed all of present-day California and Arizona as well as parts of Nevada and Utah.

California would be a portion of the United States," he proclaimed. Two days later, Sloat's forces landed at Yerba Buena, on the bay. Northern Alta California was under American control—even before official word on the declaration of war had arrived!

Southern Alta California would soon follow. Commodore Robert F. Stockton, who assumed command of the Pacific Squadron on July 15, ordered Frémont and his men to San Diego. At the same time, Stockton sent 360 of his own men to nearby San Pedro. Both groups then marched to Los Angeles, which they captured without resistance on August 13. For his part, General Castro—along with Governor Pío de Jesús Pico, a first-generation Californio who had assumed the governorship after the defeat of Micheltorena—fled the state. "California is entirely free from Mexican dominion," Stockton wrote to US Secretary of State James Buchanan.

On February 2, 1848, this situation would be made permanent. On that day, representatives from the United States and Mexico signed the Treaty of Guadalupe Hidalgo, ending the Mexican-American War. With this treaty, the United States won the war, and with it, some 500,000 square miles (1,294,994 sq km) of territory that had once belonged to Mexico. This included Alta California. With the annexation of California, the Americans' vision of "manifest destiny" had at last become a reality. The United States now stretched "from sea to shining sea."

For its part, Mexico, though certainly not happy, was not distraught by the loss of Alta California. After all, when the Treaty of Guadalupe Hidalgo was signed, fewer than twelve thousand people lived in the area, spread sparsely among sleepy missions, presidios, and pueblos. Little did Mexican authorities know that just nine days before the treaty had been signed, a carpenter named James Wilson Marshall had struck gold in northern Alta California. Marshall's discovery would spark a gold rush that would forever alter the course of American history.

Sutter's Mill

CHAPTER TWO

Discovering Gold

On July 14, 1834, Johann August Suter arrived in New York City. A German national of Swiss lineage, thirty-one-year-old Suter had set sail from Europe a few weeks prior, leaving behind his wife and five children. Why had Suter come to America? Simply put, he was on the run. Deep in debt, Suter, who had once served as a captain in the Swiss army, sought a fresh start in the New World.

Upon his arrival in the United States, Suter Americanized his name, changing it to John Augustus Sutter. Sutter quickly determined that his fortune lay to the west. First, he tried his luck in Missouri, where he worked as a trader. From there, he traveled to Santa Fe, New Mexico. Eventually, Sutter made his way to the Mexican state of Alta California by way of Oregon, Hawaii, and Alaska, arriving in 1839.

Sutter sought to establish a colony in the Central Valley near modern-day Sacramento. He would call it New Helvetia. *Helvetia* is the Latin name for Switzerland, which Sutter viewed as his ancestral homeland. First, however, he had to obtain permission from the Mexican government. Fortunately for Sutter, Governor Juan Bautista Alvarado quickly agreed to the plan. From Alvarado's point of view, Sutter's colony could serve an important role in strengthening the Mexican frontier. Alvarado granted Sutter nearly 50,000 acres (20,234 ha) of land, along with the authority "to represent … all the laws of the country, to function as political authority and dispenser of justice, in order to prevent the robberies committed by adventurers from the United States, to stop the invasion of savage Indians [who often raided the scattered coastal settlements], and the hunting and trading by companies from the Columbia [river]."

Sutter quickly began construction of his new settlement, situated at the junction of the American River (which Sutter named) and the Sacramento River. The settlement, which offered a view of the nearby Sierra Nevada, a snowy mountain range to the east, consisted of a massive adobe fort, called Sutter's Fort. The settlement also featured workshops, storage spaces, and living spaces. US Army Lieutenant William Tecumseh Sherman, who was then stationed in California but would later gain fame as a general for the Union army during the Civil War, described the settlement as follows:

> The fort … was one of adobe-walls, about twenty feet high, rectangular in form, with two-story block-houses at diagonal corners. The entrance was by a large gate, open by day and closed at night, with two iron ship's guns near at hand. Inside there was a large house, with a good shingle-roof, used as a storehouse, and all round the walls were ranged rooms, the fort-wall being the outer wall of the house. The inner wall also was of adobe. These

Captain John Sutter

rooms were used by Captain Sutter and by his people. He had a blacksmith's shop, carpenter's shop, etc., and other rooms where the women made blankets.

Initially, New Helvetia was quite prosperous. Sutter quickly achieved the grand-scale success of which he had long dreamed. Thanks in large part to labor supplied by local Natives, who were employed—or, more precisely, enslaved—by Sutter, the settlement soon boasted vast fields of grain, a 10-acre (4 ha) orchard, and some thirteen thousand cattle. Sutter's settlement was so successful, he was at last able to bring his family from Europe to live with him. His son arrived in 1844 and his wife and remaining children shortly thereafter.

Many American immigrants who entered Alta California passed through Sutter's colony, and some even stayed on. This put Sutter at odds with the Mexican government. Sutter himself would later explain, "I gave passports to those entering the country … and this (they) did not like, I was friendly with the emigrants of whom (they) were jealous. I encouraged immigration, while they discouraged it. I sympathized with the Americans while they hated them."

For their part, according to historian Robert Cleland, "these immigrants, exhausted and half-starved … found shelter, food and clothing, and an opportunity to learn something of the new land and people to which they had come."

James Wilson Marshall

One such immigrant was James Wilson Marshall. Marshall, a New Jersey native, arrived in New Helvetia in 1845. Sutter quickly hired Marshall to work as a carpenter.

James W. Marshall

A year after Marshall's arrival in New Helvetia, the United States declared war on Mexico. During the war, Marshall volunteered to serve in the California Battalion, led by John C. Frémont.

In early 1847, after Alta California had been secured by American forces, Marshall returned to New Helvetia. Sutter welcomed him back warmly. Soon, the two men entered into a partnership to construct a water-driven saw mill. Sutter wished to build a proper city and needed lumber for the project. Marshall would oversee the mill's construction and operation. In return, Sutter would give him a portion of the lumber generated by the mill.

Marshall determined that the ideal spot for the saw mill would be in Coloma. It lay 40 miles (64 km) upstream of Sutter's Fort on the American River, in the foothills of the Sierra Nevada. The area was rich in pine trees, which made for excellent lumber. Technically, it was outside the parcel of land that had been granted to Sutter. Nevertheless, in August 1847, construction of the mill began.

Unfortunately for Marshall and Sutter, it would never be completed.

Marshall Finds Gold

On January 24, 1848, James Marshall made a historic discovery. That morning, as he was examining the saw mill's **tailrace**—the ditch that drained water away from the waterwheel—he noticed some nuggets of rock glittering in the soil. Marshall later recounted, "I picked up one or two pieces and examined them attentively; and having some general knowledge of minerals, I could not call to mind more than two which in any way resembled this, sulphuret of iron, very bright and brittle; and gold, bright, yet malleable."

But which were they, sulfuret of iron or gold? To find out, Marshall "then tried it between two rocks, and found that it could be beaten into a different shape, but not broken." This seemed to indicate that Marshall had found gold. "I have found it!" Marshall famously exclaimed.

Four days after his discovery, Marshall traveled from the saw mill at Coloma to Sutter's Fort to share his discovery with Sutter. Sutter himself would later recount the story of this encounter:

> I was sitting one afternoon just after my siesta, engaged, by the bye, in writing a letter to a relation of mine at Lucern, when I was interrupted by Mr.

> [James] Marshall, a gentleman with whom I had frequent business transactions—bursting hurriedly into the room … The mere appearance of Mr. Marshall at that moment at the Fort, was quite enough to surprise me, as he had but two days before left the place to make some alterations in a mill.

Sutter continued:

> When he had recovered himself a little, he told me that, however great my surprise might be at his unexpected reappearance, it would be much greater when I heard the intelligence he had come to bring me. "Intelligence," he added, "which if properly profited by, would put both of us in possession of unheard-of-wealth—millions and millions of dollars, in fact." I frankly own when I heard this that I thought something had touched Marshall's brain, when suddenly all my misgivings were put at an end to by his flinging on the table a handful of scales of pure virgin gold. I was fairly thunderstruck.

Sutter quickly plundered his own apothecary shop for some aqua fortis, a highly corrosive solution known to dissolve most metals save gold, and applied it to Marshall's minerals. As Sutter suspected, the solution had no effect on the nuggets. Sutter then conducted further research on the matter, reading a long article about gold found in his *Encyclopedia Americana*. Finally, he was satisfied. Sutter "declared this to be gold of the finest quality, of at least 23 carats." In other words, it was 96 percent pure.

Sutter asked the crew at Coloma to keep the discovery secret for a period of six weeks. He wanted time for two reasons. First, he wanted to finish various construction projects in the settlement to ensure its continued success. Second, he wished to secure ownership of the land where the gold had been found. "The people up there promised to keep it secret so long," Sutter recalled.

This promise was soon broken, however. A worker at the saw mill shared the news of Marshall's find with a visitor, even giving him some pieces of the prized mineral as a gift. The visitor then attempted to use one of the gold pieces to purchase a bottle of brandy at Brannan & Co., the general store near Sutter's Fort. When the store's clerk questioned the piece's authenticity, the man told him of Marshall's discovery. The clerk then confronted Sutter, who was forced to confirm the story. Finally, the clerk reported this finding to the store's owner, Samuel Brannan.

Brannan, known for his business savvy, went to Coloma, assessed the situation, and promptly leased a larger storefront. He stocked his new store with every pick, shovel, and pan he could find—everything an aspiring gold prospector might need. Then, in May 1848, Brannan walked the streets of nearby Yerba Buena, which, by then had been renamed San Francisco, with a vial of gold flakes in his hand. He shouted, "Gold! Gold! Gold from the American River!" An announcement in the *California Star*, a newspaper owned by Brannan, followed. This paper would soon cease publication as its staff made for the gold fields.

Needless to say, the secret was out.

The Gold Rush Begins

Sutter sought to obtain ownership of the land on which Marshall had struck gold. To that end, he petitioned the acting governor of California, Colonel Richard Barnes Mason of the US Army. Mason denied the request. As explained by

Sam Brannan

Sam Brannan was born in Saco, Maine, in 1819. At age fourteen, Brannan moved to Ohio, where he learned the printing trade.

In 1842, Brannan joined the Church of Jesus Christ of Latter-day Saints, also called the Mormon Church. Two years later, he moved to New York City, where he launched a Mormon newspaper called the *Prophet.* He did not stay long, however. In 1846, facing growing persecution, Mormon leaders decided to relocate to the American West. While most Mormons followed church leader Brigham Young to Utah, some 235 members traveled with Brannan to Yerba Buena, arriving in July 1846.

There, Brannan launched another newspaper: the *California Star.* The next year, Brannan moved to Sutter's Fort, where he opened the only general store in the area.

When James Marshall struck gold at nearby Sutter's Mill, Brannan was fortuitously positioned to capitalize on the find. Owning the only store in the region, and having quickly stocked his shop with prospecting equipment, Brannan established a veritable monopoly. Between May 1, 1848, and July 10 of that same year, Brannan's store raked in $36,000—almost $1 million in today's money. Soon, Brannan opened more stores to serve the influx of prospectors arriving in California.

Brannan's fortune quickly grew. He became California's first millionaire. With his earnings, Brannan purchased vast tracts of land throughout California and in Hawaii. He also funded the construction of numerous fine buildings in both Yerba Buena and Sacramento and established a lucrative shipping trade. He later aided in the development of banks, railroads, and telegraph companies in California. Brannan was also elected to the San Francisco City Council, where he organized a police force of sorts.

All was not smooth sailing, however. During the Gold Rush, Brigham Young accused Brannan of pocketing tithes collected from Mormon workers to fund his own ventures. In response, Brannan is said to have told church envoys, "You go back and tell Brigham Young that I'll give up the Lord's money when he sends me a receipt signed by the Lord." Whether this statement is fact or fiction is unknown. Eventually, Brannan was kicked out of the Mormon Church.

Brannan also faced turmoil in his personal life. He developed a bad drinking habit. During a dispute over money, Brannan was shot by a contemporary, although he survived. His wife, Ann Eliza, also divorced him. The court awarded her half his assets, in cash. This, coupled with poor business decisions, drained Brannan of his fortune. On May 5, 1889, Brannan died penniless, unable to pay for his own funeral. He was seventy years old.

Lieutenant William Tecumseh Sherman, who served under Mason, "California was yet a Mexican province, simply held by us as a conquest; that no laws of the United States yet applied to it, much less the land laws or preemption laws, which could only apply after a public survey. Therefore it was impossible for the Governor to promise him (Sutter) a title to the land." Sherman noted, however, that "as there were no settlements within forty miles, [Sutter] was not likely to be disturbed by trespassers."

Sherman could not have been more wrong. As word spread about Marshall's discovery at Sutter's Mill, hordes of people descended on the area. The first wave came from Sutter's Fort. The next wave originated from San Francisco. Some of Mason's own men deserted, having been infected by gold fever. "Many of our regulars did desert," recalled Sherman. "Our servants also left us." One soldier even carried off Sherman's own shotgun, "which I prized very highly." After that came vast numbers from the eastern part of America. Finally, prospectors arrived from all over the world. In a matter of months, the land was completely overrun.

The Fates of Sutter and Marshall

Ironically, the two men responsible for the California Gold Rush, John Sutter and James Marshall, would not benefit from it in the least.

Sutter's settlement at Sutter's Fort was quickly abandoned as able-bodied workers rushed to **El Dorado**, the name given to the gold field near Coloma. Sutter's tannery was deserted. "[A] large quantity of leather was left unfinished in the vats; and a great quantity of hides became valueless as they could not be sold," Sutter recalled. He continued, "Nobody wanted to be bothered with such trash, as it was called." In addition, the mill at Coloma remained

A prospector with two burros

unfinished, so Sutter's investment was wasted. Swarms of **squatters** occupied Sutter's land, butchering his herds and destroying his crops. Left with no reasonable alternatives, Sutter himself mounted a prospecting expedition. Due to crowded conditions, this, too, was a bust. In the words of Sutter himself, "This whole expedition proved to be a heavy loss to me."

To stem his losses, Sutter deeded much of his land to his son, John Sutter Jr. On this land, Sutter Jr., along with Samuel Brannan, would found the city of Sacramento. John Sutter Sr., who would be forced to declare bankruptcy in 1852, relocated to Hock Farm, California, near the Feather River. There, his bad luck continued when his home burned to the ground. Defeated, Sutter and his wife moved back east in 1865—first to Washington, DC, and later to Lititz, Pennsylvania. In the last years of his life, Sutter continuously

Gold and Geology

Some four hundred million years ago, the rocks that would eventually form the Sierra Nevada lay submerged in a large sea. The eruption of underwater volcanoes deposited lava and minerals, including gold, on these rocks.

Over the next two hundred million years, geologic activity forced the sea floor on which these gold-encrusted rocks rested eastward. Eventually, the sea floor and the rocks collided with the North American tectonic plate, which was moving westward. Tectonic pressure pushed the sea floor and the rocks under the North American plate, where they heated up and eventually melted to produce magma. The magma then pushed its way back up, where it cooled. Much of this cooled magma became granite. As for the gold, it became concentrated in **veins** of quartz.

Movement by tectonic plates forced this granite and quartz upward, raising them to the surface to form the Sierra Nevada. Over the ensuing millennia, erosion did its work on the quartz in which the gold was encased. As the quartz crumbled, the gold was exposed. Eventually, much of this gold was carried downstream by water. In time, significant deposits of gold collected in gravel beds alongside rivers and streams. It was one of these deposits that James Marshall discovered at Sutter's Mill.

petitioned the US government for compensation for the losses he sustained during the California Gold Rush, to no avail. Sutter died on June 18, 1880. He was seventy-six years old.

Of the Gold Rush, Sutter wrote, "By this sudden discovery of the gold, all my great plans were destroyed." He continued, "Had I succeeded for a few years before the gold was discovered"—presumably to finish construction of the mill and other projects and to gain an even stronger foothold in the area—"I would have been the richest citizen on the Pacific shore; but it had to be different. Instead of being rich, I am ruined."

Marshall, too, would be ruined by the Gold Rush. Because Sutter's Mill went unfinished, he did not reap the benefits the lumber would have generated. Worse, he himself was forced off the land by the hordes of prospectors who soon arrived.

In the years that followed, Marshall drifted. He started a vineyard, but that venture failed. He then turned to prospecting, investing in a gold mine near Kelsey, California—another failure. Finally, in 1872, the California State Legislature awarded Marshall a pension to recognize his role in the California Gold Rush, which lapsed in 1878. Penniless, Marshall died on August 10, 1885. He was seventy-four years old.

As observed by James S. Brown, who had been a worker at Sutter's Mill when gold was found, "With all due respect to Capt. John A. Sutter and James W. Marshall, to whom the world has given the credit of the great find, I do believe if they had been taken out and shot to death the day of the discovery they would have suffered less, and would have met their Maker just as pure, if not more honored in this world, than to have lived and endured what they did."

Prospectors pan for gold in California.

CHAPTER THREE

The Gold Rush Begins

As word of James Marshall's discovery spread, prospectors quickly made their way to Sutter's Mill. The first wave came from Sutter's Fort. The settlement was all but abandoned as its residents sought gold. Next came prospectors from nearby San Francisco. By the end of May, just weeks after shop owner Samuel Brannan trumpeted the news that gold had been found in the American River, San Francisco had become a veritable ghost town, as its residents literally headed for the hills. One eyewitness reported that there were no more than twenty men left in the whole town. As observed by Lieutenant William Tecumseh Sherman, "nearly all business had ceased, except that connected with gold."

Then, hopeful gold seekers from San Jose, Santa Barbara, and Los Angeles arrived. Like San Francisco, these three towns became nearly deserted. As noted in the *California Star*, a newspaper in San Francisco, "Every seaport as far south as San Diego, and every interior town, and nearly every rancho from the base of the mountains in which the gold has been found, to the Mission of San Luis, south, has become suddenly drained of human beings. Americans, Californians, Indians and Sandwich Islanders, men, women and children, indiscriminately." Another newspaper, the *Californian*, complained, "The whole country from San Francisco to Los Angeles, and from the sea shore to the base of the Sierra Nevadas, resounds with the sordid cry of gold, GOLD, GOLD! while the field is left half-planted, the house half built, and everything neglected but the manufacture of shovels and pickaxes." Eventually, prospectors from Oregon, Mexico, and even Hawaii began to arrive.

Many early prospectors enjoyed great success. Often, a single day's yield equaled between ten and fifteen times their normal daily wage back home. Lieutenant Sherman observed, "We heard of men earning fifty, five hundred, and thousands of dollars per day, and for a time it seemed as though somebody would reach solid gold." One small group of these early prospectors pulled some $120,000 worth of gold from the Feather River, which would be worth approximately $3 million today.

Then came a lull. It took time for news of Marshall's discovery to reach the eastern part of the United States. Although the telegraph had long been developed and tested—in 1844, inventor Samuel Morse demonstrated its use in the chambers of the US Supreme Court, sending the oft-quoted message "What hath God wrought?" to a colleague in Baltimore—the first transcontinental telegraph lines had yet to be built. (A transcontinental telegraph connecting San Francisco with the East Coast would not be completed until 1861. This was even later than the completion of the Atlantic telegraph line that connected the United States with Europe, in 1858.) In 1848, when Marshall struck gold, news to and from California still traveled by ship or by horseback, and as such, it took time to arrive at its destination.

Finally, on September 15, 1848, a small notice appeared in the *New York Herald*:

> INTERESTING FROM CALIFORNIA—We have received some late and interesting intelligence from California. It is to the 1st of July … It relates to the important discovery of a very valuable gold mine. We have received a specimen of the gold.

Initially, this news was met with some skepticism. When this same news reached London on October 10, the editor of the *London Times*, doubtful of its veracity, buried the story on page four, noting, "We need hardly observe that it is necessary to view these statements with great caution." A few weeks later, the same wary editor wrote, "We must hear more of this El Dorado before we bestow upon it our serious consideration. There are some textures which will not bear many weeks washing, and the gold mines of the Sacramento may be one of them."

Finally, on December 5, 1848, US President James K. Polk confirmed Marshall's finding during a special address to Congress. "The accounts of the abundance of gold in that territory are of such an extraordinary character as would scarcely command belief were they not corroborated by the authentic reports of officers in the public service," Polk said. One of the officers in question was US Army Lieutenant Lucien Loeser, who, under the direction of Colonel Mason, had traveled from San Francisco to Washington, DC, by ship and horseback to deliver the news—and, with it, "the first piece of gold ever discovered in this Northern part of Upper California found by J.W. Marshall at the Saw Mill of John A. Sutter."

Suddenly, skepticism changed to excitement, even mania. As reported by the *New York Herald*, stories of gold in California "set the public mind almost on the highway to insanity." Almost immediately, companies formed to transport prospectors and supplies to California. All across the United States and even around the globe, people quit their jobs, packed up their homes, and headed for California—often incurring great debt in the process. On December 12, the *New York Herald* noted, "The gold mania rages with intense vigor, and is carrying off its victims hourly and daily." In the words of Lieutenant Sherman, "Then began that wonderful development, and the great emigration to California, by land and by sea, of 1849 and 1850."

Newcomers Arrive

In 1849, some eighty thousand prospectors—often called Argonauts, a nod to the famous band of heroes in Greek mythology who sought a Golden Fleece—arrived in California. About half these people, referred to forevermore as **forty-niners**, arrived by sea. The other half came overland via the California Trail.

Most of these forty-niners were men who had left their families back east. Some arrived in California with their wives and children in tow, however. All of these travelers were driven by a feverish optimism, no doubt convinced they would strike it rich. One prospector, Franklin Buck, who sailed to California from the East Coast, wrote to his sister, "One fellow ... threw his last five dollar piece ashore. Says he, 'I'm going where there is plenty more!'"

The journey by sea was long. Ships departed from the East Coast, sailed around the southern tip of South America, and then traveled north to San Francisco. On average, the trip, which usually covered more than 18,000 nautical miles

(33,336 km), took two hundred days—more than six months. From San Francisco, prospectors then embarked on yet another journey by boat, this time up the Sacramento River to the gold fields, some 125 miles (201 km) inland.

The first of these sea voyagers arrived in San Francisco on February 28, 1849. These brave souls departed for California long before President James K. Polk confirmed that gold had been found in the area. Soon, the harbor was jammed with ships. In the twenty-five years preceding Marshall's discovery, an average of just 25 vessels landed in San Francisco—in other words, about one ship visited the port per year. In 1849 and 1850, that number increased to 793 and 803, respectively.

Prospectors who took the overland route to California were at a distinct disadvantage. Due to the weather, they were unable to start their journey until early April, with most arriving in California by early September. On average, the journey took between 120 and 160 days. Most traveled by covered wagon, although many came by mule or horse, and some even by foot. Their numbers were staggering. One immigrant, a fourteen-year-old girl named Sallie Hester, wrote, "As far as [the] eye can reach, so great is the migration, you see nothing but wagons … a vast army on wheels."

The route of this "vast army" was the California Trail. The trail began at the Missouri River, crossed Nebraska and Wyoming, and turned northwest into Idaho. From there, it turned south, meandering through the northwest corner of Utah and into Nevada, and eventually into northern California. The first part of the trail, across the Great Plains, was flat and relatively easygoing. But as travelers entered the Rocky Mountains, challenges mounted. The terrain was nearly impassable. Those who made it across faced an even more challenging environment: the desert. Beyond that lay

Why Is Gold Valuable?

For thousands of years, humanity has prized gold. Due to its extreme beauty, gold has long been used for decorative purposes. It has also been used as **currency**, or money. Indeed, both the Egyptians and Romans used gold as their primary medium of exchange. But why?

Of the 118 elements in the periodic table, just eight emerge as contenders for currency: the noble metals. Why these metals? First, they barely react to other elements, meaning they won't corrode or explode. Second, they are relatively rare. Some, however, are too difficult to extract, and others are so rare that they are nearly impossible to find. That leaves just gold and silver as viable options for currency. It's no surprise that both of these elements are used for just this purpose. And the fact that both elements—particularly gold, whose color is distinctive—are considered beautiful no doubt increase their value in people's minds.

Of course, in and of itself, gold holds no real value. It can't be eaten or drunk or used for protection from rain, snow, wind, heat, or cold. Still, gold has been an important part of human society for thousands of years and will likely remain so for some time to come.

A wagon train on the California Trail

the towering Sierra Nevada. Not surprisingly, many died along the way.

Adding to the travelers' difficulties was the threat of disease. Cholera plagued the prospectors as they crossed the plains. In the mountains, they contracted mountain fever. Pneumonia, typhoid fever, and diphtheria were also a concern. Many travelers succumbed to these illnesses.

Of course, it wasn't just Americans who made for California. People came from around the globe. In particular, large numbers of Chinese sailed for San Francisco. Interestingly, when traveling by sea, China was closer to the California coast than the Eastern United States! At first, most of these Chinese immigrants avoided the gold fields. Instead, they worked as laborers, carpenters, and cooks. Eventually, some Chinese did take up the search for gold, although they

San Francisco: Boom Town

When James Marshall discovered gold in the foothills of the Sierra Nevada in January 1848, San Francisco, some 140 miles (225 km) to the southwest, was nothing more than a small settlement of just one thousand people. Soon, there would be even fewer. As residents rushed to the Sierra Nevada in search of gold, the town was left all but empty.

The next year, the town experienced a rebirth. By the end of 1849, its population had grown to five thousand people. At the end of 1850, that number had exploded to thirty thousand.

Why this phenomenal growth? Simple. San Francisco was the landing point for prospectors arriving by sea. These people needed food, lodging, and supplies before setting off to find gold. To respond to this demand, enterprising locals set up taverns, boarding houses, hotels, shops, and other businesses. One such local was Levi Strauss, who opened a dry goods store. Now, Levi's is a famous brand of jeans. Another was Phillip Armour, who opened a butcher shop. This grew to become Armour Foods.

Many of these businesses were housed in abandoned ships or in wood-framed canvas tents. Often, they caught

San Francisco, circa 1850, two years after the discovery of gold

fire. Large portions of San Francisco burnt to the ground not once, not twice, but *six times* between 1849 and 1852! The fifth fire—which some believed was set deliberately by local gangs—destroyed some two thousand buildings over eighteen blocks in just ten hours. The flames were so bright that they could be seen from as far away as Monterey.

usually did not work an area until after it had been abandoned by white prospectors.

The Life of the Prospector

When these prospectors—some eighty thousand in 1849 alone and thousands more in the years that followed—reached the gold fields in the Sierra Nevada, life was primitive at best. There was no infrastructure in place to support this influx of people. As a result, most of these newcomers lived in wagons, tents, or shanties. Many slept on the ground, "with pine leaves and blankets for bedding," according to Lieutenant William Tecumseh Sherman. Eventually, they built more substantial dwellings, although these were often nothing more than shacks. For these miners, nature held the upper hand. Conditions were harsh and a turn in the weather could mean death. One in twelve forty-niners perished.

At first, the area where miners searched for gold was small: in and around Coloma, where James Marshall struck gold. That area was quickly stripped bare, however. From there, miners searched upstream in an attempt to find the source of the gold, the quartz from which the gold had originated. Much of this quartz was still in the bedrock, which lay underground. In time, miners discovered this source, or **lode**, which they called the Mother Lode. The Mother Lode was an area between 1 and 4 miles (1.6 to 4.3 km) wide and 120 miles (193 km) long, extending from Georgetown in the north to Mormon Bar in the south. It contained gold deposits that were nearly 50 feet (15 m) thick and a few thousand feet long.

Who owned the land under which this gold lay dormant? At first, the gold fields, a 60 by 200 mile (97 by 322 km) area in the Sierra Nevada, existed on public lands owned by the United States. This region was larger than the Mother Lode

Stocking Up

Typically, prospectors who came by sea bought the supplies they needed in San Francisco—but what of the prospectors who arrived via the California Trail? Typically, they stocked up at Sutter's Fort, many of them at Brannan & Co.

The prospector's list of supplies was long. Of course, each prospector needed a shovel, pick, and pan. In addition, each of them typically bought a blanket, a tent, and food, such as bacon, beef jerky, beans, flour, sugar, tea, and coffee. If they had a little extra money, they might also spring for a lamp, kettle, baking pan, hatchet, hoe, and pail.

These items didn't come cheap. At Brannan & Co., common mining pans sold for between $8 and $16 ($215 and $430 in 2015). For this reason, merchants made far more money than most miners during the California Gold Rush.

because gold from that lode often traveled downstream. However, because the United States had acquired California just months before the onset of the Gold Rush, there were few rules in place, and even fewer ways to enforce them.

For the first prospectors, gold was essentially free for the taking. They paid no licensing fees and no taxes. Later, prospectors were required to "stake a claim." To do so, a prospector would claim an area in which he wanted to search for gold by driving stakes into the ground.

The prospector would also register the claim with the local authorities and pay a small fee. Eventually, as land speculators took over, the prices of claims climbed. In 1850, one group of men paid $450, more than $12,600 today, for a claim just 60 feet (18 m) long. Prospectors could hold only one claim at a time. If one claim yielded nothing, then the prospector abandoned it to stake a new one.

Often, prospectors partnered up to increase their chances of finding gold. Sometimes, hundreds of miners collaborated in this way, forming large camps. Miners hastily built new camps in areas where they struck gold, only to abandon them when the deposits of the precious mineral dwindled. Often, these camps—which were lawless places, with names like Rough and Ready and Hangtown—had their own saloons and gambling houses. There, after long days of backbreaking labor, the miners cut loose. They sang, danced, drank, played cards, and, occasionally, fought.

Eventually, towns formed to serve the growing population of miners. Typically, these towns boasted restaurants, saloons, stores, barber shops, tailors, a doctor's office, a lawyer's office, a bank, and, eventually, a church. One such town was Columbia, founded in 1850 when prospectors struck gold nearby. For a time, it was California's second-largest city, its population peaking at twenty thousand.

Food in the gold fields was, in a word, unappetizing. In part, this was because store owners charged outrageous prices for food. A single egg or a slice of bread cost $1 each—almost $27 in 2015. Therefore, miners often resorted to eating, in the words of author Paul Robert Walker, "rancid bacon, beans, and old beef jerky." Fruits and vegetables were scarce, and many miners contracted scurvy, a disease characterized by swollen, bleeding gums, loosening teeth, and bleeding into the skin and mucous membranes.

Perhaps worse than the harsh environment, the lousy food, and the threat of illness—not to mention the arduous nature of the work itself and the lawless nature of the camps—was the loneliness these miners felt. Most had left their families behind in search of their fortune. Many wrote letters home. In time, if funds allowed, some sent for their wives and children.

Mining Techniques

Initially, gold was so abundant in California that prospectors could simply pick it up with their hands, as James Marshall did at Sutter's Mill. Soon, however, prospectors began to **pan** for gold in rivers and streams. With panning, the prospector used a wide, shallow pan to scoop up gravel alongside (or under) a river or stream. He then agitated the pan in the water. Any gold in the gravel, being denser than the surrounding minerals, would settle in the bottom of the pan, while the remaining minerals would wash away.

This approach, while effective, was quite labor-intensive. Soon, prospectors developed a new approach, which involved using a machine called a **rocker**. This simple wooden device resembled a baby's cradle. In the words of Lieutenant Sherman, it was "open at the foot, and at the head a plate of sheet-iron or zinc, punctured full of holes. On this metallic plate was emptied the earth, and water was then poured on it from buckets, while one man shook the cradle with violent rocking by a handle." With a rocker, three men could work together to process larger amounts of gravel. One man dug the gravel and deposited it into a bucket. The second man carried the bucket to the rocker. The third man poured water into the rocker to wash the gravel, rocking the machine back and forth to separate the gold from the gravel. This, too, was backbreaking work. One

Gold Rush Ghost Towns

Like mining camps, mining towns were quickly constructed when prospectors found a new vein of gold and quickly abandoned when that vein ran dry. An example of one such abandoned town, called a ghost town, was Coloma, where James Marshall first struck gold.

After Marshall's discovery, Coloma, whose name derives from the Nisenan tribe's word *cullumah*, meaning "beautiful," was quickly overrun by prospectors in search of riches. Indeed, for a time, Coloma was *the* destination for anyone seeking gold. By 1849, the town, which had grown to contain some three hundred buildings, including stores, hotels, business, saloons, and gambling houses, had a population of ten thousand.

Soon, however, miners found richer gold veins elsewhere in the Sierra Nevada. They abandoned Coloma for new towns, such as Placerville, Georgetown, Diamond Springs, and Columbia. By 1870, just two hundred residents remained. For all practical purposes, Coloma became a ghost town.

prospector reported carrying three hundred buckets of dirt in one day. This yielded $75 in gold, which would be more than $2,000 in 2015, to be split evenly among the three men. "Not bad," the prospector noted, "but not as good as the work should have produced." After rockers came long toms. These were similar to rockers but larger, and able to process even more gravel.

Other, more invasive methods soon followed. One was **hydraulic mining**. With this technique, miners directed water from a high-pressure hose at the hillside, reducing it to a heap of gravel. This loosened gravel, presumably containing gold, was then diverted to a **sluice**—a series of long, narrow boxes filled with water for processing the gravel. Any gold in the gravel quickly settled on the bottom to be collected by miners. This method was very destructive to the environment. For this reason, it was outlawed in 1884.

Another invasive method, called **hard-rock mining** or quartz mining, involved extracting gold directly from the surrounding rock, which was usually quartz. To achieve this, miners first dug up the quartz, then used a machine called a stamp mill to crush it. Then, chemicals such as mercury were applied to the remaining pieces to extract the gold. These methods were more expensive. As such, they were typically employed only by larger mining companies who hired miners to do the job.

Between 1848 and 1853, prospectors used these methods to remove some 370 tons (336 metric tons) of gold from the gold fields of California, a haul worth more than $16 billion in today's money.

What Happened to the Gold?

What did prospectors do with the gold they found? At first, much of the gold found by prospectors was simply used

Stagecoaches like this one were used to transport gold from California back to cities on the East Coast.

to pay for supplies, food, lodging, or entertainment. Many gambled. The merchants who received gold as payment from prospectors then used it to purchase goods from suppliers, such as ship captains who imported merchandise from abroad.

Eventually, local businessmen built banks. There, prospectors could exchange gold for banknotes, which were locally accepted paper money. By 1849, companies began minting coins using gold found by prospectors. These were accepted as currency. In 1854, another player entered that market: the US government. That year, it opened the San Francisco Mint.

Some gold was transported back east. One company that transported gold from California to the East Coast was Wells Fargo. Typically, gold was transported by **stagecoach**. The driver stored the gold behind him in a locked box. Next to him sat a guard armed with a shotgun (the origin of the still-popular phrase "riding shotgun"). Despite these precautions, these vehicles were frequent targets for bandits.

The Gold Standard

At the time of the California Gold Rush, the US government adhered to the **gold standard**. That is, it tied the value of its currency—the dollar—to a specific amount of gold. (At the time, this was not an established practice. The United States formally adopted the gold standard in 1900.) Countries that adhered to the gold standard kept stores of gold. This gold had a fixed value. In the United States, one ounce of gold equaled $20.67. The country then printed money based on how much gold it kept.

The discovery of gold in California was a monetary shock. It disrupted this system by increasing the supply of gold, and as a result, the supply of money. This caused prices to go up. Higher prices made US exports more expensive, which caused a deficit in the country.

Although the gold standard conferred long-term price stability, short-term shocks—like the one experienced by the United States as a result of the Gold Rush—made it less attractive over time. For this and other reasons, namely the standard's inflexibility, the United States abandoned the gold standard in 1973. Still, there are many who call for its reinstatement. Some are attracted by its simplicity. Others view it as an effective way to anchor prices worldwide.

Prospectors during the California Gold Rush

CHAPTER FOUR

The Tide Turns

For the first prospectors who reached the gold fields in 1848, gold mining was often a lucrative endeavor. Because much of the area in which gold could be found was public land, there were few rules with regard to where prospecting was allowed. In addition, much of the gold was easily found, often just resting on gravel beds alongside streams and rivers. The gold that was found on the surface of these gravel beds was called **placer gold**. And although whole communities, like San Francisco and Sutter's Fort, emptied out as prospectors made for the gold fields, there were still relatively few miners to compete with in those early days. Historians estimate that perhaps four thousand prospectors searched for gold during 1848. Because their numbers were relatively few and because so much of the gold was easily accessible, many of these early prospectors struck it rich.

That started to change in 1849, as more and more prospectors came to California in search of gold. That year, an estimated eighty thousand miners arrived in the area. Yet more came the next year and the year after that. The gold fields became crowded with miners.

Just staking a claim became difficult. By 1850, much of the land had been snatched up by speculators, who charged high prices for mining rights. Even when a miner *could* stake a claim, in all likelihood, any placer gold on that plot had already been found. That meant using more labor-intensive and expensive mining techniques, like a rocker or a long tom, or performing hydraulic mining or hard-rock mining. In the early days, an individual could pan for gold and expect some return for his efforts, but as time passed, only larger mining companies that hired teams of miners using expensive equipment could expect to turn a profit.

Of course, even if these more advanced techniques were used, there was still no guarantee of finding gold. A great number of prospectors, particularly those who arrived later in the Gold Rush, would be disappointed. Some returned home. Others, lacking funds for their return trip, remained in California, destitute.

Ultimately, the mining of gold in California would peak in 1852. That year, miners hauled in 3.9 million **troy ounces** (121 million grams) of the metal. By 1865, production would fall to one-quarter of this amount.

The Squatters' Riot of 1850

Unable to stake a claim due to high prices charged by land speculators, many prospectors were forced to live as squatters—that is, to occupy land to which they were not legally entitled. Many of these squatters lived in the area surrounding Sacramento. The city, founded in 1848 by John Sutter Jr. and Samuel Brannan, had quickly grown to boast some ten thousand residents.

In October 1849, a logger named Z.M. Chapman, who had built a log cabin on a parcel owned by a land-speculation company, was sued by that company. The company, unable to provide definitive proof of ownership, lost the case. Inspired by Chapman's success, another man, Charles L. Robinson, built his own shack on private land. In addition, Robinson formed the Sacramento City Settlers Organization, a group devoted to squatters' rights.

Charles L. Robinson. Robinson, the founder of the Sacramento City Settlers Organization

Emboldened, squatters began holding public meetings in the spring of 1850. In these meetings, squatters swore to defend their lands. They also formed a militia to challenge land speculators. In retaliation, speculators demolished a squatter-built fence in the area.

In May 1850, a squatter named John T. Madden was charged with unlawful occupation of land owned by John Sutter. This time, the squatter, who claimed that because Sutter had received the land from the Mexican government, the land grant was invalid, lost his case. On August 8, Madden was evicted from his property. Two days later, under Robinson's direction, fellow squatters rallied to Madden's defense. "A large meeting of the squatters took place," noted William M. Gwin, who would later serve in the US Senate. Gwin continued, "They resolved that as [California was not yet a US state], the laws created by the Legislature were of no force, and that they would resist until

Gold Rush Bandits

Not everyone who struck gold during the California Gold Rush went through the trouble of pulling it from the ground. Some simply stole it, a task made simpler by the arrival of the .44-caliber Colt Dragoon revolver, which became available in 1848.

One such bandit was Reelfoot Williams. He frequently robbed miners of their gold. In 1851, Williams was arrested for highway robbery, but he beat the charge. In an amusing twist, Williams attempted a holdup the next day, only to discover that his intended victim was the judge who had acquitted him. Williams let the judge go and instead robbed the next man who came along.

In 1852, Williams joined forces with another bandit, Rattlesnake Dick, and three other thieves. Together, these crooks held up stagecoaches transporting gold. Three members of the gang were soon killed during a shootout with a sheriff and his men, but Williams and Rattlesnake Dick escaped. In the end, however, they too met an untimely end. Rattlesnake Dick was stabbed to death in 1853, and Williams was shot by a rival during the 1860s.

Another famous figure who pulled similar jobs was Joaquin Murrieta—although whether he was considered a bandit or a Mexican patriot depends largely on one's point of view. Over the years, his story became a mixture of fact and legend. Indeed, Murrieta may have been the inspiration for the fictional character of Zorro, who was dreamed up by author Johnston McCulley in the early twentieth century. Historian Susan Lee Johnson notes, "So many tales have grown up around Murrieta that it is hard to disentangle the fabulous from the factual." There seems to be a consensus, however, that "Anglos drove him from a rich mining claim, and that, in rapid succession, his wife was raped, his half-brother lynched, and Murrieta himself horse-whipped."

Seeking revenge against the attackers, Murrieta assembled a gang. This gang killed six of the white settlers who had assaulted Murrieta and his family. In addition, the gang attacked random settlers and wagon trains, allegedly killing many. To some, particularly those of Mexican descent, Murrieta was not a "gringo eater" but a Mexican Robin Hood of sorts. Nevertheless, California authorities considered Murrieta and his gang so dangerous that they formed the California State Rangers to hunt them down. In July 1853, a group of these Rangers located the outlaws. In the ensuing firefight, three members of Murrieta's gang were killed, including Murrieta. To prove he was dead, officials cut off Murrieta's head, preserved it in a jar of alcohol, and displayed it at a saloon.

death any mandate coming from any of our courts." Some of these squatters were later arrested and placed in jail.

On the morning of August 14, Robinson and a fellow squatter named Joseph Maloney mobilized the squatters' militia and marched through Sacramento. In Gwin's words:

> This morning they organized to the number of one or two hundred, who had muskets and small arms, and aided by a large number ready to assist them, all armed, they marched through the streets in regular military style, their leader on horseback, with sword; went to several places from which they had been ejected and took possession; and then wended their way to the prison-ship, to release the two of their number that were imprisoned on yesterday.

In response, the mayor of Sacramento, Hardin Bigelow, quickly gathered his own force to confront the militia. Bigelow ordered Robinson's men to stand down. Instead, they fired. In the ensuing battle, both Bigelow and Robinson were injured. Five people died—among them Maloney and two civilian bystanders.

There would be one more attack on the squatters, by Sacramento Sheriff Joseph McKinney. McKinney led an assault on a squatter camp east of Sacramento. McKinney and three squatters were killed. The conflict between squatters and speculators would soon wind down, however. Eventually, the land speculation that had so incensed the squatters came to an end.

And what of Bigelow and Robinson? Bigelow stepped down as mayor to nurse his wounds, but died shortly thereafter of cholera. Robinson was more fortunate. His wounds healed. Although he was indicted for murder, he did not go to trial. A popular figure, Robinson was elected to the California State Legislature, in which he served from 1851 to 1852. In 1860, he was elected the first governor of Kansas.

California Becomes a State

One argument cited by the squatters was that because California was not a US state, the laws created by the US Legislature did not apply. This would soon change.

When the United States acquired California, the region's status was unclear. It was not a state because the US Congress had not granted it statehood. Nor was it considered a formal US territory. Instead, it was ruled by military governors. Among these was Colonel Richard Barnes Mason, under whom Lieutenant William Tecumseh Sherman served.

This arrangement was highly unusual. Typically, when the United States acquired new parcels of land, those parcels were initially deemed formal territories—for example, the Louisiana Territory. Eventually, after meeting certain criteria, including a population of at least sixty thousand people, they would be granted statehood. Often, this took several years to achieve. Sometimes, however, new acquisitions were granted immediate statehood, as was the case with Texas in 1845.

California, however, was neither of these. But why? Simply put, Congress could not agree on whether California would allow slavery or be a Free State. Lawmakers from the South wanted to extend slavery to the Pacific coast, while those from the North did not.

Nevertheless, within California, a movement for statehood quickly arose. This movement, led by General Bennett C. Riley, who assumed the military governorship of California in 1849, was largely in response to California's quickly growing population, which had been spurred almost entirely by the Gold Rush. These newcomers, most of whom were already American citizens, wanted better representation in Congress.

As a first step, Riley called for a Constitutional Convention in June 1849. Delegates for the convention were elected by secret ballot on August 1. In September 1849, the delegates—forty-eight in all—convened in Monterey. Most were American settlers who had arrived in California before 1846, although a few were native-born Californios. During the convention, which lasted forty-three days, the group drafted a state constitution. This document was similar to the US Constitution. With regard to slavery, the California Constitution outlawed it, except as punishment. This was in part because prospectors wanted to avoid competition from slave owners in the gold fields.

On November 13, 1849, Californians ratified their new constitution by popular vote. Soon after, a provisional government drew out county boundaries and elected a governor, state senators, and state representatives. This government also selected a state capital: San Jose. (This would turn out to be temporary. A new state capital, Vallejo, was chosen in 1852. In 1853, the capital would move again, this time to Benicia. Finally, in 1854, lawmakers selected Sacramento. It remains the capital of California to this day.) Despite all this preparation and organization, California's status in the Union remained unclear.

That changed on September 9, 1850, when US lawmakers passed the Compromise of 1850, a series of bills meant to resolve the confrontation between northern and southern states regarding slavery. Among other things, the Compromise of 1850 granted California statehood. California, the thirty-first state in the Union, would be a Free State.

Because there was still no telegraph line from the East

CONSTITUTION

of the

STATE of CALIFORNIA.

We the People of California

Article I.

Declaration of Rights.

Section 1.

Sec. 2.

Sec. 3.

Sec. 4.

Sec. 5.

Sec. 6.

The California Constitution, written in 1849

Coast to California, news of this development did not reach California right away. Settlers on the Pacific coast, including the tens of thousands of prospectors who had by then flocked to the region, would not learn of their new status until the middle of October. When at last the news broke, settlers erupted in a spontaneous celebration that lasted for weeks.

A Census Takes Stock

California's booming population was one key reason it was granted statehood, but just how many people were in California? In 1846, at the outbreak of the Mexican-American War, the population of Alta California, then a Mexican state, was quite small. Fewer than 10,000 Californios, 1,300 US citizens, and 500 Europeans lived in the area, most in the northern part of the state. As for the Native population, it was unknown, although estimates put it at as high as 150,000 people.

In 1850, the US government conducted a **census**. This revealed that there were more than 120,000 citizens in California, not counting any Native Americans. Interestingly, fewer than 10,000 of these were women. A second census in 1852 revealed that the population had grown even larger, to 200,000, and just 20,000 were female. It would not be until the 1950 census nearly one hundred years later that the ratio of men to women would approach one to one.

This growth was due partially to the fact that the price of passage to California by sea had lowered significantly, to just $200. The trip had become shorter, too. No longer were passengers required to sail around the southern tip of South America. Now, they could disembark on the eastern coast of Panama, cross that country by horseback (or, later, by railroad) to the Pacific, and catch a second ship to San Francisco. A journey that once took two hundred days now lasted just forty. Of course, it was not always smooth sailing. On one crossing from California to New York, the SS *Central America* sank, taking with it 3 tons (2.7 t) of California gold.

The Effects of the Gold Rush on Indigenous Populations

While the number of white settlers in California dramatically increased, the Native American population began to fall. As more and more prospectors arrived in California, Native Americans found themselves crowded out, driven from their traditional hunting, fishing, and food-gathering grounds. Denied access to their historical means of survival, many Native Americans starved. Others died of diseases brought by these newcomers, like smallpox, influenza, and measles, against which they had no natural immunity. Still others were simply killed by the encroaching settlers, who viewed them as merely obstacles to be overcome in their search for gold.

Often, those Native Americans who were spared were forced into slavery, despite California's status as a Free State. This practice was made possible by the 1850 passage of the Act for the Government and Protection of Indians. This law allowed settlers to arrest Native Americans for minor offenses such as loitering or public intoxication. If the charged individual could not pay the fine, the person who arrested him could put him to work or even sell him to someone else. So, for example, as noted by author James Parins, "If an Indian was arrested on charges of drunkenness and could not pay his fine, a white rancher could pay the amount levied by the court and then set the prisoner to work until the debt was paid." Parins continued, "The Indian had no voice in setting the terms of this transaction, those details being left to the judge and the rancher." This law also enabled settlers to purchase Native children, placing them in servitude.

Not surprisingly, tensions ran high between the indigenous people and settlers. There was frequent fighting, with a pattern of escalating violence. In one example, in 1852, a band of Wintu people killed a white settler. In retaliation, settlers slaughtered 150 Wintu. Just three Natives, all of them children, survived the attack. Ironically, the Wintu killed were not the same band who had killed the settler.

Eventually, the state of California hired vigilante groups to protect settlers from Native Americans. However, genocide might be a better way to describe the mission of these groups. Indeed, the first governor of California, Peter H. Burnett, noted, "That a war of extermination will continue to be waged between the two races until the Indian race becomes extinct, must be expected." Burnett

Attacks on Chinese Miners

Native Americans were not the only population who faced attacks by white settlers. As resources dwindled, American miners also attacked foreigners, particularly those from China, in an attempt to drive them out. Many Chinese were physically assaulted, and some were even killed.

Interestingly, in the early days of the California Gold Rush, Chinese workers, who initially avoided labor in the gold fields in favor of other work, were warmly welcomed. In his book *The Story of California from the Earliest Days to the Present*, published in 1924, author Henry K. Norton wrote, "Here were men who would do the drudgery of life at a reasonable wage when every other man had but one idea—to work at the mines for gold. Here were cooks, laundrymen, and servants ready and willing. Just what early California civilization most wanted these men could and would supply." Norton continued, "The result was that the Chinaman was welcomed; he was considered quite indispensable."

Eventually, some Chinese did take to the gold fields, although according to Norton, "They were careful not to antagonize … whites by prospecting ahead of them." As a result, these Chinese miners were widely tolerated—

Chinese prospectors pan for gold in California.

until, that is, gold became scarce. As more and more white prospectors met with disappointment in the gold fields, said Norton, "they turned upon the men of other races who were working side by side with them and accused them of stealing their wealth." Norton continued, "They boldly asserted that California's gold belonged to them.

The cry of 'California for the Americans' was raised and taken up on all sides."

In 1852, the California State Legislature took action. Rather than protecting foreign prospectors, however, it passed the Foreign Miners' License law. This law levied a monthly tax of $3 (about $80 in 2015) on Chinese miners, an amount that represented half a Chinese miner's earnings. If a Chinese miner could not (or would not) pay the tax, his property was confiscated and sold. Sometimes, "delinquent" Chinese miners were stabbed or shot.

An 1854 California Supreme Court ruling officially demoted Chinese residents of California to second-class citizens. The case in question centered on three white men who had been convicted of killing a Chinese man, based on testimony provided by Chinese witnesses. The court overturned the ruling, citing a California law that prevented African Americans, Native Americans, and all other people of color from testifying in court. The judges ruled that the Chinese, like these other subjugated populations, were "a race of people whom nature has marked as inferior and who are incapable of progress or intellectual development beyond a certain point."

continued, "While we cannot anticipate the result with but painful regret, the inevitable destiny of the race is beyond the power and wisdom of man to avert." Sometimes, these miners killed as many as fifty Natives in a single day.

Not surprisingly, according to historian R. David Edmunds, "The Native American population plummeted from approximately 150,000 on the eve of the Mexican-American War to less than 30,000 twenty-five years later." After the California Gold Rush, the Native American population was reduced by 80 percent.

The End of the Gold Rush

For all practical purposes, the California Gold Rush ended in 1855. By then, the Mother Lode had been all but tapped out. Still, stragglers remained. Finally, in 1859, the discovery of silver in nearby Nevada, the so-called Comstock Lode, caught their attention. In a mad scramble, these and other prospectors made for Nevada to stake their claims.

Gold would still be mined in California, even after the Gold Rush. Discoveries of new lodes and deposits would continue. However, none of these would draw the interest and excitement that characterized those mad years between 1848 and 1855.

A view of San Francisco, circa 1860. The city grew by leaps and bounds as a result of the California Gold Rush.

CHAPTER FIVE

The Effects of the Gold Rush

The California Gold Rush lasted from 1848, when James Marshall struck gold at Sutter's Mill, until 1855, when the Mother Lode in the Sierra Nevada was spent. It had a tremendous impact on hundreds of thousands of people, on the state of California, and on the United States, both in the short term and the long term.

What were the effects of the Gold Rush? The event profoundly changed the lives of all those prospectors who searched for gold, as well as their families. It also greatly affected the course of history in the state of California, the United States, and the entire world. There were cultural impacts, economic impacts, and environmental impacts.

It's Personal: How the Gold Rush Affected Individuals

The California Gold Rush affected specific individuals in various ways. Some people, particularly those first prospectors to reach the gold fields in 1848, enjoyed

The Next Big Finds

While the California Gold Rush ended in 1855, it was followed by many others that again sparked gold fever.

One gold rush ignited in Deadwood, South Dakota, in 1875. Roaming miners who had previously served under the famous Lieutenant George A. Custer discovered placer gold in Deadwood Creek. Word of their find quickly spread. By early 1876, all the land around the creek had been claimed by prospectors. Still, more came.

Like their California counterparts, prospectors in Deadwood—which quickly grew into a boomtown—knew that the placer gold had originally come from a lode of quartz formations under the earth. They set out to find them. In April 1876, three miners named Fred Manuel, Moses Manuel, and Alex Engh discovered a gold-bearing section of rock near present-day Lead, South Dakota. Interestingly, the gold was not tightly encased in the quartz, making it much easier to remove. This area was but a small part of what would become the most productive gold vein in American history. In fact, over the next 125 years, this area would produce 10 percent of the world's gold supply.

In 1896, yet another gold rush sparked, this time in the Klondike region of the Yukon in northwestern Canada. It began when a Native American named Skookum Jim and two white settlers called Dawson Charlie and George Carmack discovered placer gold in a tributary of the Klondike River. Throngs of local prospectors descended on the site, which they named Bonanza Creek. Nearby Eldorado Creek yielded even more treasure. In fact, almost all of the first claims on Eldorado Creek—forty in all—produced at least a half-million dollars in gold.

In the case of the Klondike, those men who already lived in the area found the most gold. That's because outsiders did not learn of the find until nearly a year later, when two steamships carrying eighty miners and 3 tons (2.7 t) of Klondike gold arrived in Seattle and San Francisco. Their arrival prompted a stampede, as some one hundred thousand prospectors rushed to the Far North. Fewer than half would arrive at their destination, which involved a voyage by steamship from the Pacific Northwest to Alaska followed by a 600-mile (966 km) trip by trail and river to the gold fields. Of those who did complete the journey, only four thousand or so actually struck gold. By 1899, the Klondike Gold Rush had ended, almost as suddenly as it had begun.

Although these gold rushes were significant, and each resulted in the same type of boom and bust seen in California, neither spawned a permanent significant migration to new territory as the California Gold Rush did.

Some prospectors stayed in California after the Gold Rush to farm the fertile land.

tremendous success. Indeed, a lucky few became wealthy beyond their wildest dreams. Others, especially those who arrived later, were not so fortunate. The unluckiest died. The slightly less tragic, having failed to strike gold, simply found themselves destitute.

Although some so-called forty-niners eventually returned east, a great many stayed in California. Some remained simply because they were too poor to secure passage home, but more stayed because they had become quite taken by the area. The land was more than just lovely; it was fertile. Therefore, many prospectors stayed on to farm the land, having been rejoined with their families. Indeed, the large-scale agriculture that followed became known as California's "second Gold Rush." As noted by economist Gerald D. Nash, "Without a doubt, the Gold Rush was the major stimulant of California agriculture in the 1850s." He continued, "Thousands became small farmers, viticulturists, fruit growers, and dairy farmers. Others became sheep and cattle raisers."

The Impact on California

Thanks to the Gold Rush, California would undergo tremendous changes in a period of just seven years. The most obvious of these was the explosion in the region's population.

The California Gold Rush unleashed a massive migration, drawing hundreds of thousands of settlers to the region. Where before, the Native Americans vastly outnumbered settlers of European or Mexican descent, that quickly changed. By the end of the Gold Rush, California would boast more than two hundred thousand settlers. Meanwhile, the indigenous population would be decimated.

This population explosion was significant for many reasons, not least of which that it spurred the US Congress to grant statehood to California in 1850, far earlier than it would have otherwise. Even before this, however, settlers in California developed a system of governance. They convened a constitutional convention, wrote a state constitution, and held elections.

The new Californians also chartered several cities and towns to accommodate the growing population, with the necessary roads, schools, churches, and other infrastructure. These included cities like Columbia and Sacramento as well as mining towns like Coloma and Placerville. At the same time, existing settlements, like San Francisco, grew exponentially. In 1848, San Francisco had just 1,000 residents. Two years later, that number had grown to 30,000 people. By 1870, it had ballooned to 150,000.

Of course, this growth had a tremendous environmental impact. So, too, did the activities of the miners themselves. As noted by author Kathy Weiser, "As miners continued to invent faster, more destructive methods of finding gold,

Certain mining techniques ravaged the land.

the land was ravaged. Hillsides were washed away in torrents of water, and towns downstream were inundated by immense floods of mud. Water supplies were poisoned with mercury, arsenic, cyanide, and other toxins. Grand forests of oak and pine were leveled for mining timbers."

The legacy of the California Gold Rush can be found everywhere: It's represented in the state seal by a miner. It's also reflected in the state motto: "Eureka," which is Greek for "I have found it," the very words spoken by James Marshall upon striking gold. And of course, the origin of the state's nickname, "The Golden State," is self-explanatory. Allusions to the Gold Rush also appear on signs that mark state highways, which are shaped like a miner's spade, and in the name of the National Football League team in San Francisco, the 49ers.

California Dreaming

As a direct result of the Gold Rush, California became the thirty-first state in the Union. This had significant repercussions in the ongoing national conflict regarding slavery. Because California was admitted as a Free State, it gave abolitionists the edge they needed—one that would come in handy in the years to come, as the slave states seceded from the Union and the American Civil War began.

The California Gold Rush also had a less tangible effect on the course of American history. In a sense, it helped to form Americans' vision for the future. As noted by historian H.W. Brands, "[This] golden dream ... became a prominent part of the American psyche only after Sutter's Mill."

Lured by this new frontier, one made so attractive by the California Gold Rush, more and more Americans moved west. This migration was soon facilitated by Congress's passage of the Pacific Railroad Act in 1862. This law paved the way for the construction of the Pacific Railroad, which spanned from Sacramento, California to Council Bluffs, Iowa. From Council Bluffs, the Pacific Railroad connected to existing tracks, which went all the way to the Atlantic Ocean.

Work on the project, financed in part with Gold Rush money, commenced in 1863. Some laborers began laying tracks in Sacramento and worked east. Others started in Council Bluffs and moved west. (Later, the railroad would extend to San Francisco.) In May 1869, the two sets of tracks converged at Promontory Summit, Utah. In a special ceremony, railroad president Leland Stanford, who had himself migrated to California during the Gold Rush and become a successful merchant, used a silver hammer to pound a golden railroad spike into the ground.

With the advent of the Pacific Railroad, Americans could

Workers celebrate the completion of the Pacific Railroad in May 1869.

travel safely from New York to California in an astonishing eight days. The railroad did more than just reduce travel time, however. It united the country. As noted in the New York Times, thanks to the Pacific Railroad, "The inhabitants of the Atlantic seaboard and the dwellers on the Pacific slopes are henceforth emphatically one people."

Worldwide Ripples

The effects of the California Gold Rush spread far beyond the borders of California and even those of the United States. They rippled worldwide.

The most significant of these were the economic effects. Thanks to the population explosion that ensued in California during the Gold Rush, huge markets opened up for farmers in Chile, Australia, and Hawaii. The Chinese also capitalized on the Gold Rush, manufacturing clothing and even prefabricated homes for the newly settled region.

Californians weren't just consumers, however. They were also producers. As noted, the Gold Rush played a large part in the development of California agriculture. All those farmers, viticulturists, fruit growers, dairy farmers, and sheep and cattle raisers sold their goods not only to the fellow Americans but also to markets up and down the Pacific Coast and even the Pacific Rim. According to Nash, "They found that California farm products enjoyed considerable success in Asia, as did beef and mutton."

"I have found it," James Marshall said when he struck gold, and indeed he had. But neither Marshall nor Sutter nor anyone else could have imagined the incredible changes that find would bring.

Chronology

400,000,000 BCE The rocks that will form the Sierra Nevada lie undersea. On these rocks, gold is eventually deposited after the eruption of underwater volcanoes.

September 28, 1542 Juan Rodriguez Cabrillo "discovers" present-day California (although indigenous people have lived there for thousands of years). He claims the region for Spain.

June 1579 Sir Francis Drake lands in northern California. He appropriates the territory for England.

July 1769 Spain builds its first mission in California, in San Diego.

1810–1821 The Mexican War for Independence; Mexico wins and declares its independence from Spain.

1846–1848 The Mexican-American War. The United States prevails, taking control of California.

January 24, 1848 James Marshall discovers gold at Sutter's Mill. Marshall and John Sutter attempt to keep the find secret.

February 2, 1848 Representatives from the United States and Mexico sign the Treaty of Guadalupe Hidalgo, ending the Mexican-American War.

May 1848 In San Francisco, Samuel Brannan sparks the California Gold Rush when he holds up a vial of gold and shouts, "Gold! Gold! Gold from the American River!"

September 15, 1848 A report of Marshall's discovery appears in a New York City newspaper.

December 5, 1848 US President James K. Polk confirms the discovery of gold in California, igniting "gold mania."

February 28, 1849 The first forty-niners arrive in San Francisco.

June 1849 General Bennett C. Riley, the military governor of California, calls for a Constitutional Convention.

September 1849 Delegates gather for the Constitutional Convention. During the convention, the delegates draft a state constitution.

November 13, 1849 Californians ratify the state constitution by popular vote.

August 14, 1850 The Squatters' Riot erupts in Sacramento.

September 9, 1850 California becomes the thirty-first state in the Union.

1851 California exports $34,492,000 in gold—$967,142,000 in 2015.

1852 California exports $45,587,803 in gold—$1,278,264,000 in 2015; Sutter declares bankruptcy; the California State Legislature passes the Foreign Miners' License law, requiring Chinese miners to pay a monthly tax of $3.

1853 California exports $56,390,812 in gold—$1,581,176,000 in 2015. This represents the peak of the California Gold Rush.

1854 Sacramento becomes the permanent capital of California; the US Mint opens in San Francisco; California exports $51,429,101 in gold—$1,335,233,000 in 2015.

1855 California exports $44,640,090 in gold—$1,117,620,000 in 2015; the California Gold Rush effectively ends.

1859 Miners find silver in Nevada, spurring a silver rush.

1861 The first transcontinental telegraph line is completed. Californians can now receive news from the East Coast in minutes rather than months.

1869 Workers complete the Pacific Railroad. Passengers can now travel from New York City to California in just eight days.

1875 Prospectors find gold near Deadwood, South Dakota, spawning a new gold rush.

1896 Gold is found in the Klondike, prompting the Klondike Stampede.

Glossary

annex To officially take control of a region of land.

Californio One of the Spanish-speaking people of Alta California.

census An official count of an area's population.

circumnavigate To travel completely around something, such as the Earth.

conquistador A Spanish explorer.

currency Something that is used as money.

El Dorado Spanish for "The Golden," meaning a land of great wealth or opportunity.

forty-niners People who migrated to California in 1849 in search of gold.

Franciscan A member of a group of Catholic priests who traveled the world to perform missionary work.

gold standard A monetary standard in which the basic unit of currency equals a set quantity of gold.

hard-rock mining A mining technique that involves extracting gold directly from the surrounding rock by digging it up, crushing it, and applying chemicals to it to remove the gold.

hydraulic mining A mining technique in which miners direct water from a high-pressure hose at the hillside, reducing it to gravel, which is then diverted to a sluice for processing.

Jesuits An order of Catholic priests who traveled the world to perform missionary work.

lode A deposit of minerals, such as gold.

manifest destiny A philosophy that espouses that it is America's duty to expand its territory and spread its way of life.

mission A settlement that is built to gain a foothold in an area as well as to convert the Native people to Christianity.

missionary A person who goes to another country to do religious work, such as convert Native people to a religion.

pan A mining technique in which a wide, shallow pan is used to scoop up gravel alongside (or under) a river or stream and then agitated in the water to sift out the gold.

placer gold Gold found on the surface of a gravel bed.

presidio A Spanish fort.

prospector One who searches, or prospects, for minerals such as gold. Also called a miner.

pueblo A town built by the Spanish to support their missions and presidios.

rancho A large land grant issued by Spain to a prospective settler in Alta California.

rocker A simple wooden device used to process gravel and find gold.

sluice A series of long, narrow boxes filled with water for processing gravel to extract gold.

squatter A person who occupies land to which he or she is not legally entitled.

stagecoach A carriage pulled by horses to transport passengers and goods.

tailrace A ditch that drains water away from the waterwheel in a mill.

troy ounce A unit of measure applied to precious metals. It is equivalent to just over 31 grams.

vein A long, narrow opening in rock filled with minerals such as gold and silver.

Further Information

Books

Brands, H.W. *The Age of Gold: The California Gold Rush and the New American Dream.* New York: Anchor, 2003.

Dolnick, Edward. *The Rush: America's Fevered Quest for Fortune.* New York: Little, Brown and Company, 2014.

Maxwell-Long, Thomas. *Daily Life During the California Gold Rush.* Santa Barbara, CA: Greenwood, 2014.

Websites

American Experience: The Gold Rush

www.pbs.org/wgbh/amex/goldrush/index.html

This site offers links to articles about key people in the California Gold Rush, a timeline, a map of mining sites, and more.

Gold Rush: California State Library

www.library.ca.gov/goldrush

Find links to resources—from photos to articles to letters and more—about the California Gold Rush.

San Francisco: Gold Rush

www.sfmuseum.org/hist1/index0.1.html#gold

Visit this site for links to first-person accounts of the California Gold Rush, including excerpts from John Sutter's diary and an account by William Tecumseh Sherman.

Museums

California State Mining and Mineral Museum

Located in historic Mariposa, in the foothills of the Sierra Nevada, this museum hosts the official mineral collection of the state of California—some thirteen thousand objects in all. You can also view exhibits about how gold was mined during the California Gold Rush.

The Gold Rush Trail

This walking trail through San Francisco offers glimpses of life during the Gold Rush.

Marshall Gold Discovery State Historic Park

This park, located where James Marshall discovered gold, boasts a replica of Sutter's Mill and twenty historic buildings. A guided tour is available and visitors can even pan for gold.

Bibliography

"American Experience: The Gold Rush." PBS. Accessed July 19, 2015. http://www.pbs.org/wgbh/amex/goldrush/index.html.

Avey, Tori. "Food of the California Gold Rush." The History Kitchen. Accessed July 19, 2015. http://www.pbs.org/food/the-history-kitchen/food-california-gold-rush.

Bordo, Michael D. "Gold Standard." Library of Economics and Liberty. Accessed July 19, 2015. http://www.econlib.org/library/Enc/GoldStandard.html.

Brands, H.W. *The Age of Gold: The California Gold Rush and the New American Dream.* New York: Anchor, 2003.

"Building the Transcontinental Railroad." Digital History. Accessed July 19, 2015. http://www.digitalhistory.uh.edu/disp_textbook.cfm?smtID=2&psid=3147.

"California." 50States.com. Accessed July 19, 2015. http://www.50states.com/california.htm#.VZsDHmdRGZM.

"California American Indian Facts." Native American Indian Facts. Accessed July 19, 2015. http://native-american-indian-facts.com/California-American-Indian-Facts/California-American-Indian-Facts.shtml.

"California Becomes the 31st State in Record Time." History. Accessed July 19, 2015. http://www.history.com/this-day-in-history/california-becomes-the-31st-state-in-record-time.

"California Gold Discovery." Coloma California. Accessed July 19, 2015. http://www.coloma.com/california-gold-discovery.

"The California Gold Rush, 1849." Eyewitness to History. Accessed July 19, 2015. http://www.eyewitnesstohistory.com/californiagoldrush.htm.

Dúran, Narcisco. "Secularization of the Missions." Digital History. Accessed July 19, 2015. http://www.digitalhistory.uh.edu/disp_textbook.cfm?smtID=3&psid=540.

"Foreign Miner's Tax." Oakland Museum of California. Accessed July 19, 2015. http://explore.museumca.org/goldrush/curriculum/gamsaan/foreigntax2.html.

Friedman, Morgan. "The Inflation Calculator." Accessed July 6, 2015. http://www.westegg.com/inflation.

Gold Nugget. The National Museum of American History. Accessed July 19, 2015. http://americanhistory.si.edu/collections/search/object/nmah_741894.

"History, Legends & Lore: Gold Mining in the Black Hills." Black Hills Visitor. Accessed July 19, 2015. http://blackhillsvisitor.com/featured-articles.html?pid=879&sid=962:Gold-Mining-in-the-Black-Hills.

"History of the Telegraph." History Wired. Accessed July 19, 2015. http://historywired.si.edu/detail.cfm?ID=324.

"John Sutter and California's Indians." HistoryNet. Accessed July 19, 2015. http://www.historynet.com/john-sutter-and-californias-indians.htm.

"Juan Rodriguez Cabrillo." 2004. Encyclopedia.com. Accessed July 19, 2015. http://www.encyclopedia.com/topic/Juan_Rodriguez_Cabrillo.aspx.

"Juan Rodriguez Cabrillo." San Diego History Center. Accessed July 19, 2015. https://www.sandiegohistory.org/online_resources/cabrillo.html.

"New Perspectives on the West." PBS. Accessed July 19, 2015. http://www.pbs.org/weta/thewest/index_cont.htm

Nash, Gerald D. "A Veritable Revolution: The Global Economic Significance of the California Gold Rush." *A Golden State: Mining and Economic Development in Gold Rush California.* Ed. James J. Rawls and Richard J. Orsi. Berkeley, CA: University of Berkeley Press, 1999.

Norton, Henry K. *The Story of California from the Earliest Days to the Present.* Whitefish, MT: Kessinger Publishing, 2010.

Ojibwa. "California's War on Indians, 1850 to 1851." Accessed July 19, 2015. http://nativeamericannetroots.net/diary/1862.

"Old West Legends: The California Trail—Rush to Gold." Legends of America. Accessed July 19, 2015. http://www.legendsofamerica.com/we-californiatrail.html.

Pretty, Francis. "Sir Francis Drake's Famous Voyage Round the World." Accessed July 19, 2015. http://legacy.fordham.edu/halsall/mod/1580Pretty-drake.asp.

Putnam, John. "The First Stagecoach Robbery in the California Gold Rush." Examiner.com. http://www.examiner.com/article/the-first-stagecoach-robbery-the-california-gold-rush.

Rowlatt, Justin. "Why Do We Value Gold?" BBC.com. Accessed July 19, 2015. http://www.bbc.com/news/magazine-25255957.

"Sam Brannan." SierraFoothillMagazine.com. Accessed July 19, 2015. http://www.sierrafoothillmagazine.com/brannan.html.

"Sir Francis Drake." Royal Museums Greenwich. Accessed July 19, 2015. http://www.rmg.co.uk/explore/sea-and-ships/facts/explorers-and-leaders/drake

"Squatters Riot San Francisco City 1850." YesterYearsNews. Accessed July 19, 2015. https://yesteryearsnews.wordpress.com/2009/04/14/squatters-riot-sacramento-city-1850.

The Virtual Museum of the City of San Francisco. Accessed July 19, 2015. http://www.sfmuseum.net.

Walker, Paul Robert. *All About America: Gold Rush and Riches.* New York: Kingfisher 2011.

"What Was the Klondike Gold Rush?" National Park Service. Accessed July 19, 2015. http://www.nps.gov/klgo/learn/goldrush.htm.

Yerger, Rebecca. "Sam Brannan: Pioneer, Dreamer, and Scoundrel." InsideNapaValley.com. Accessed July 19, 2015. http://napavalleyregister.com/inv/lifestyles/sam-brannan-pioneer-dreamer-and-scoundrel/article_600ee514-3ae9-11e0-8969-001cc4c002e0.html.

Index

Page numbers in **boldface** are illustrations. Entries in **boldface** are glossary terms.

About the Author

Kate Shoup has written more than thirty books and has edited hundreds more. When not working, Kate loves to watch IndyCar racing, ski, read, and ride her motorcycle. She lives in Indianapolis with her husband, her daughter, and their dog. To learn more about Kate and her work, visit www.kateshoup.com.